CANALS

Graham Rickard

Wayland

Topics

Airports
Ancient peoples
Archaeology
Bridges
Canals
Castles
Costumes and Clothes
Earthquakes and Volcanoes
Energy
Fairs and Circuses
Farm Animals
Ghosts and the Supernatural
Great Disasters
Helicopters
Houses and Homes
Inventions
Jungles
Maps and Globes

Money
Musical Instruments
Peoples of the World
Photography
Pollution and Conservation
Prisons and Punishment
Railways
Religions
Robots
Shops
Spacecraft
Stamps
Television
The Age of the Dinosaurs
The Olympics
Trees of the World
Under the Ground
Zoos

All the words that appear
in **bold** are explained in the
glossary on page 30.

Cover The Corinth Canal in Greece

Editor: Rosemary Ashley

First published in 1987 by
Wayland (Publishers) Ltd
61 Western Road, Hove
East Sussex BN3 1JD,
England

British Library Cataloguing in Publication Data
Rickard, Graham
  Canals. – (Topics).
  1. Canals – Juvenile literature
  I. Title   II. Series
  398'4   HE526

  ISBN 1–85210–090–7

Phototypeset by Kalligraphics Ltd, Redhill, Surrey
Printed and bound in Belgium
by Casterman S.A., Tournai

Contents

What are Canals?   4

The History of Canals   11

Building a Canal   18

Modern Canals   25

Glossary   30

Books to Read   31

Index   32

What are Canals?

Ever since people first saw how a floating log could be used to carry them over water, the world's oceans and rivers have been used as an important method of transport, especially for heavy goods.

This ancient dug-out canoe, made from a hollowed-out tree trunk, was recovered from the mud of the River Thames.

An aqueduct in Sweden. It carries the calm waters of the canal over a fast-running river.

But there are often problems with natural waterways. Rivers may flood in winter and dry up in summer. In some places, especially hilly areas, there are either no rivers or they are too shallow or flow too quickly for boats to use. Rivers can be made straighter, wider or deeper to take boats, but sometimes it is cheaper and more convenient to dig an artificial waterway, called a **canal**.

An irrigation canal provides water for fruit trees in California, USA.

There are several different types of canal. Small **irrigation** canals are dug to carry water to dry farmland, while drainage canals drain water from wet, marshy ground. Canals large enough to carry people and cargoes are called navigation canals. These can be used by boats, **barges**, and even the largest ocean-going ships.

Canals are an efficient way of moving large amounts of heavy cargoes, such as timber, steel and coal. Many of the world's inland cities, for example Chicago, Manchester, and Liège in Belgium, have become important ports because of canals that connect them to the sea.

Some canals, such as the Suez Canal in the Middle East and the Panama Canal in Central America, save time and money by providing a 'short-cut' which greatly shortens sea journeys. In some cities, like Amsterdam and Venice, canals are

often the main form of transport. They are used as 'streets', with boats taking the place of cars and buses.

Boats are the main form of transport in Venice as most of the 'streets' are canals.

A narrowboat is held steady by ropes while water rushes into the lock as the sluices are opened.

Unlike rivers, canals do not flow. They are built level to stop the water running away. When the land is not level, the canal is built in sections, called **pounds**, at the different levels. Where two pounds meet, the different levels of water are separated by a **lock**.

A lock is a large water-box with gates at each end. The level of water in the lock is controlled by opening flaps called **paddles**, which allow water to run into or out of the lock through **sluices**. On modern locks, the paddles are worked by electricity, but on older locks the **paddle gear** has to be turned by hand, using a special lock-key or **windlass**.

When a boat passes through a lock system, the water in the lock has to be at the same level as the water outside the lock where the boat is, before the heavy gates are opened, either electrically or by pushing a lever called a 'balance beam'. The boat enters the lock and the gates are closed behind it so that the water level can be raised or lowered to the same height as that in the next section of canal. The gates at the other end are then opened and the boat can continue its journey.

When the water in the lock has reached the right level, the heavy gates are opened by pushing long levers, and the boat is ready to leave the lock.

Boats are hauled up a steep slope on an 'inclined plane' on the Marne-Rhine Canal in France.

In hilly areas, there may be several locks placed close together in a **flight**, or they may even be joined in a **staircase** to carry boats up and down steep slopes. Another way of raising or lowering boats in hilly areas is to lift them in a tank, either vertically in a **boat lift**, or on a slope with rails called an **inclined plane**.

The History of Canals

Archaeologists in Iraq have discovered remains of canals that are 6,000 years old. But these waterways were fairly short, primitive **cuts** without any locks.

The Chinese invented the modern **pound-lock** system almost a thousand years ago. They built

The Great Canal in China is over 700 years old. It is still in use today.

many locks along the Great Canal of China, which ran 1,780 km from Peking to Hangchou, and was completed in the thirteenth century.

In Europe, the Romans built lengths of simple, single-level canals. However, pound-locks, with swinging gates to hold back the water, were not used until the Italian artist and engineer Leonardo da Vinci (1452–1519) designed and built such locks for the Duke of Milan. The Languedoc Canal, completed in 1681,

Traditional narrow-boats carry coal along the Grand Union Canal in Hertfordshire, England.

connected the Mediterranean Sea with the Atlantic Ocean and saved ships a voyage of over 1,600 km. Similar canals were built throughout Germany and Holland.

But the modern age of canals started in eighteenth-century England. The growing towns and factories of the Industrial Revolution needed a cheap way of carrying food, raw materials and finished goods from one place to another. The roads at that time were very rough and pack-horses were the only way of transporting heavy goods in winter.

The Duke of Bridgewater wanted a cheap way of moving coal from his mines to the factories and homes of Manchester. He asked the engineer, James Brindley, to design and build a canal. Completed in 1761, the canal was a great success and many companies followed the Duke's example by digging a network of canals all over Britain.

The Bridgewater Canal, built by James Brindley for the Duke of Bridgewater, was opened in 1761.

Fleets of **narrowboats**, carrying every kind of cargo, were soon travelling around the new inland waterways and this allowed trade and industry to grow as never before. Factories and whole new towns sprang up on the canal banks, and the canal companies made fortunes from the **tolls** that they charged for the use of the waterways.

The people who lived and worked on the gaily-painted narrowboats formed a community with their own way of life and their own traditions.

Wide modern canals can be used by large freight barges. These are more economical than trains or trucks for carrying heavy cargoes.

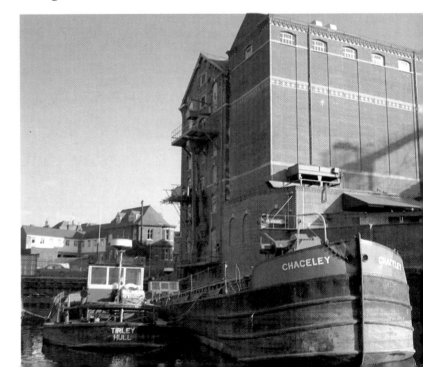

A tiny cabin sometimes provided the only living space for entire families on narrowboats.

They worked long hours for little money and the whole family helped. The boatman's wife often assisted in steering the boat by pushing the **tiller** to turn the **rudder**, or she opened and closed the many lock gates. Even young children used to help by walking on the **tow-path** behind the horse which pulled the boat on a long rope.

The whole family lived in the tiny cabin at the back of the boat, which had a stove, furniture and beds packed into the cramped space.

A diesel-engined tug can tow a number of butties.

When steam and diesel engines replaced the horse, each narrowboat could pull a barge, called a **butty**, behind it allowing more cargo to be carried.

In the nineteenth century, the coming of the faster railways almost killed off the English canal trade and many waterways were either filled in or abandoned. Those that remain are busy once again, but are used more for pleasure than for business purposes.

In Britain many narrowboats have been converted to pleasure craft. This boat takes tourists on the Avon Canal and is pulled by a horse on the towpath.

Building a Canal

Before work can start on any canal, the whole area has to be **surveyed**. In the early days of canal building, engineers usually did this on horseback, using **theodolites** and other instruments to measure the levels of the surrounding countryside. From these levels, they planned the exact route of the

Some of the detailed plans drawn up for the construction of a canal in 1798.

canal and the position of each lock. Early canals usually followed a crooked line to avoid hills and other obstacles. Later canals were made much straighter, because the engineers used locks, deep cuttings and tunnels through hilly areas.

In the days before machines, digging a canal was a tremendous task. Groups of men moved around the countryside digging the canals by hand, using only picks, shovels and wheelbarrows. These men were called navigators or '**navvies**', and they lived a hard, rough life.

A viaduct and deep cutting, during the construction of the Manchester Ship Canal in the nineteenth century.

Once they had dug the canal, they lined it with a thick layer of 'puddle', a mixture of wet clay that stopped the water seeping through the sides. They also built locks, bridges, and all the other buildings that you can see on a canal.

A team of navvies at work repairing the Regent's Canal in London in the early 1900s.

One of the most difficult and dangerous jobs was to dig a tunnel through a steep hill. First, the navvies dug several vertical shafts from the top of the hill down to the level of the canal. Then they dug tunnels sideways from each shaft until they joined up. As they worked, their only light was provided by candles. When they came up against solid rock, they had to blast it clear using gunpowder. Where the earth was too soft to make a safe tunnel, teams of bricklayers lined the whole passage with thousands of bricks before any water could be let through.

Where the canal crossed over a river or valley, the navvies had to build an **aqueduct**. Some of these aqueducts are wonderful feats of engineering. The one at Pontcysyllte in North Wales, for example, is 307 m long and carries a canal 37 m above the River Dee.

The famous Pontcysyllte Aqueduct in North Wales is a masterpiece of canal engineering.

Heavy shipping traffic on the Schleswig-Holstein Canal in West Germany.

Modern canals are longer, wider and deeper than the early ones. By using modern machinery, such as bulldozers, dumper-trucks and great tunnelling drills, it has become much quicker and easier to build them. Huge machine-made cuttings, such as the 12.8 km Gaillard Cut on the Panama Canal, allow canals to pass through even the steepest mountains. For locks big enough to take the largest ocean-going ships, massive steel lock gates are built and lifted into place by crane.

Even when a canal is completed, regular maintenance work is needed to keep it in good working condition. Dredging boats make sure that the canal remains deep enough by dragging up mud and silt from the canal-bed. To prevent damage to the sides of the canal, **piles** are driven deep into the banks

A dredging ship clears the bed of the Suez Canal, making sure that it is deep enough for large ships to pass through.

A repair team at work on a drained canal bed.

to hold back the earth. Ice-breakers help to keep the waterways clear in winter, and weeds and overhanging trees are regularly cut back to prevent them obstructing the boats. Most canals also have skilled workers who are kept busy repairing locks, fitting new gates and replacing loose stones and bricks on the many bridges, tunnels and aqueducts.

Modern Canals

Although the great English canal trade was almost killed off by the coming of railways and improved roads, inland waterways still provide an important form of transport throughout much of the world.

Modern canals are built to handle large ships, and barges which can carry as much as 700 tonnes of cargo. Entire new waterways have been made by digging canals to join rivers and lakes.

In Holland, the giant locks on Neder Rijn are always busy with heavy traffic.

Amsterdam, like Venice, is a city of canals, and boats are used for carrying cargoes, sightseeing and as homes.

In Sweden, for example, the Göta Canal is actually made up of several different canals that link a chain of rivers and lakes right across the country. The entire journey of 610 km from Stockholm to Göthenburg takes three days. Holland has over 8,000 km of canals, and Amsterdam itself has over one hundred canals. Many of its citizens live on colourful houseboats, and the city's flower-market, called the *Singel*, is a collection of floating rafts.

In North America, canals were more important than stagecoaches in opening up the West. Today, the St. Lawrence Seaway, which joins the Great Lakes, takes ships 3,750 km inland from the Atlantic and is an important trade route. Houston, in Texas, is over 80 km from the coast, but is still one of America's busiest ports, thanks to the Houston Canal which links it to the Gulf of Mexico.

Two of the world's most famous canals provide quick 'short cuts' across land to join seas and oceans. The Panama Canal cuts across Central America, saving ships a long and difficult journey around South America. The Suez Canal links the Mediterranean Sea with the Red Sea, providing a shorter route between Europe and the Far East. Before it was built, ships had to travel around the whole continent of Africa.

New canals are constantly being built. In Romania, a 62.4 km canal was recently completed. It links the River Danube to the Black Sea and saves 380 km on the journey through central Europe.

As well as providing an efficient form of transport, canals have other uses too. They can supply fresh water to farms, factories and cities. In addition, more and more people are enjoying canals in their holidays and leisure-time.

On the Panama Canal, large boats are pulled through the Gatun Lock by powerful locomotives, which run on railway 'towpaths'.

Canals are enjoyed by many people, including this weekend angler.

A floating holiday on a converted narrowboat or barge can be very relaxing, and there is always something interesting to see on a canal. Many types of plants, fish, birds and animals thrive on or in the inland waterways.

Canals are as useful today as they have ever been. Modern industry still needs large quantities of such raw materials as coal, oil and steel, and transporting them by canal is the cheapest, if not the quickest way of moving these heavy goods over long distances.

As the world's natural supplies of oil and gas begin to run out, the price of fuel is steadily rising. Consequently, it seems as though more and more cargoes will be carried by canal in the future. Canals are already helping to solve the energy crisis: in the Soviet Union, the waters of the Moscow-Volga Canal are being used to drive **turbines** to make electricity.

Scientists are always looking for new sources of energy and perhaps we shall soon see solar-powered barges on our waterways, as road, rail and air transport become more expensive.

A specially designed barge carries cars to Le Havre for export. Canals are ideal for such large cargoes.

Glossary

Archaeologist A person who finds and studies the buildings and objects made by ancient civilizations.

Aqueduct A bridge-like structure, that carries a waterway over an obstacle, such as a valley or road.

Barge Flat-bottomed boat for carrying cargoes.

Boat lift A way of lifting or lowering boats vertically in a water-tank.

Butty An unpowered narrowboat which is pulled behind another boat.

Canal A man-made channel that holds water.

Cut A section of canal.

Flight A group of locks built close together to climb a hill.

Irrigation The watering of dry farmland by means of narrow water-channels.

Inclined plane A way of lifting or lowering a boat in a water tank, by hauling it up and down rails on a steep slope.

Lock A water-box, with gates at either end. The amount of water can be adjusted to allow boats to travel from one level to another on a canal.

Narrowboat A traditional long canal boat (21m long, 2m wide) with a small cabin for the boatman and his family.

Navvies Short for 'navigators', the name given to the labourers who built the early canals by hand.

Paddle Movable opening in a lock to allow water in or out, to adjust the level.

Paddle gear System of cogs, rods, etc. which opens the paddle.

Pile Lengths of wood, metal or concrete driven into the edge of a canal to protect its banks.

Pound-lock A section of canal between two locks.

Rudder Flat wooden or metal board beneath the rear of the boat, which moves under the water to steer the vessel.

Sluice Water-channel for filling or emptying a lock.

Staircase Several locks, one above the other, which are joined together on a steep hillside.

Survey To inspect the countryside, measuring its levels, before building a canal.

Theodolite A surveying instrument that measures the different levels of the land.

Tiller The wooden or metal lever at the rear of the boat, which turns the rudder to steer the craft.

Toll Charge made for using a section of canal owned by a company.

Tow path Path along one side of the canal for the horse that towed the boats.

Turbine A machine that produces electricity when it is turned by water or steam.

Windlass Handle-shaped key needed to turn the paddle gear on a lock.

Books to Read

A Source Book of Canals, Locks and Canal Boats by H. McNight (Ward Lock Ltd, 1974)

Canals by Christine Vialls (A & C Black, 1975)

Canals by Jane Dorner (Wayland, 1977)

Canals are My World by J. M. Pearson (Bryce, 1986)

Canals in Colour by A. Burton (Blandford, 1974)

Canal People by Anthony J. Pierce (A & C Black, 1978)

Inland Waterways by Patrick Thornhill (Methuen, 1959)

Pictorial History of Canals by J. Gladwin (Batsford, 1977)

Picture acknowledgements
The illustrations in this book were supplied by: Hugh McKnight 4, 7, 10, 12, 13, 15, 16, 18, 19, 20, 21, 24, 25, 29; Graham Rickard 8, 9, 14, 28; ZEFA cover picture, 5, 6, 11, 17, 22, 23, 26, 27.

Index

Amsterdam 7, 26
Aqueducts 5, 21, 24

Barges 6, 25, 28
Boat lift 10
Bridges 20, 24
Bridgewater, Duke of 13
Brindley, James 13
Butties 16

Canals
   Avon 17
   Bridgewater 13
   Danube-Black Sea 27
   drainage 6
   Göta 26
   Grand Union 13
   Great Canal of China 11, 12
   Houston 26
   irrigation 6
   Languedoc 12
   Manchester Ship 19
   Marne-Rhine 10
   Moscow-Volga 29
   navigation 6
   Neder Rijn 25
   Panama 6, 22, 27
   Regents 20
   St Lawrence Seaway 26
   Schleswig-Holstein 22
   Suez 6, 23, 27
Canal companies 14

Canalboat people 14–15
Cargoes 6, 16, 25, 29

Dredging ship 23
Dugout canoe 4

Engineers 18, 19, 21

Great Lakes 26

Holiday craft 17, 28
Houseboats 26

Inclined plane 10
Industrial revolution 12–13

Leonardo da Vinci 12
Lock-gates 8, 9, 15, 19, 20, 22, 24
Locks 8, 9, 10, 12, 19, 20, 22, 24
   pound-locks 11, 12

Narrowboats 5, 13, 14, 16, 17, 28
Navvies 19

Paddle-gear 8
Pounds 8

Railways 17, 25

Shipping 5, 6, 7, 8, 9, 10, 12, 15,
   22, 25, 26, 27
Sluices 8

Toll-fees 14
Tow-paths 15, 17
Tunnels 19, 21

Venice 7

Wildlife 28
Windlass 8